BRITAIN TODAY

INDUSTRY

EWAN McLEISH

WAYLAND

TITLES IN THE SERIES

THE ENVIRONMENT
FARMING
INDUSTRY
TOURISM

Series editor: **Sarah Doughty**
Book editor: **Penny McDowell**
Series designer: **John Christopher**
Production controller: **Carol Titchener**
Consultant: **Suzannah Lansdell, Manager, Business
Programmes, The Environment Council**

First published in 1995 by **Wayland (Publishers) Limited**
61 Western Road, Hove, East Sussex, BN3 1JD, England.

© Copyright 1995 **Wayland (Publishers) Limited**

British Library Cataloguing in Publication Data
McLeish, Ewan
Industry. – (Britain Today Series)
I. Title II. Bull, Peter III. Series
338.0941

ISBN 0-7502-1536-4

Picture Acknowledgements

The publishers would like to thank the following for supplying the photographs
for this book: Neill Bruce 24; Ecoscene 9; Mary Evans Picture Library 6, 7
(both), 20; Stuart Oliver Limited 10; Popperfoto 40; Still Pictures 43; Tony
Stone Worldwide cover, 4, 5, 12, 14, 16, 23, 27, 28 (both), 29, 30, 30–31, 34,
36–37, 38, 39, 41; Zefa 8, 18, 26, 35, 45; Michael Zinn 45; TENCEL photograph
reproduced by kind permission of TENCEL Fibres Europe (Courtaulds Fibres);
photography by Max Bradley; Marketing Consultants: CMT International 33.
The illustrations on pages 11 and 13 were supplied by Peter Bull.

Typeset by White Design
Printed and bound in England
by B.P.C. Paulton Books

CONTENTS

INTRODUCTION

▲ Coal mining – much of Britain's wealth was built on this primary industry; now the future of coal is uncertain.

Almost every society depends on what it grows and what it makes. It may make products to meet its own needs, or to create wealth by selling them to other societies. As societies develop, most become more dependent on making and selling products, that is, on manufacture and trade. At the same time, the means of production – their industries – become more complex. Such societies are said to be industrialized. Britain is an example of a highly industrialized society.

Britain has a **mixed economy**. Some industries operate on a free enterprise basis, that is, free from influence or ownership by the state; others are under direct government control. In recent years, many of the industries which were under government control (nationalized), such as British Gas, have been 'sold off' (privatized) and are now owned and controlled by **shareholders**.

FACT BOX

THE THREE MAIN SECTORS OF INDUSTRY

- **the primary sector – where resources or raw materials are obtained, for example, mining, quarrying and drilling for oil;**
- **the secondary sector – where primary products are used to produce or manufacture goods, for example, steel, electronics, cars and chemicals;**
- **the tertiary sector – where services are provided, for example, banking, selling (retailing), advertising, insurance, tourism and telecommunications.**

All industries require energy in one form or another and the supply of energy is a major industry in itself.

Businesses may vary in size from one or a few employees to large national or multinational companies, employing tens of thousands of people, such as ICI or the petrochemical industries. Most are limited companies with shares either available to the general public (Public limited company or Plc) or owned by the directors or managers of the business itself (Limited or Ltd).

In 1955, manufacturing accounted for 42 per cent of the workforce. In 1994, this figure had dropped to 20.3 per cent. In contrast, the service industries now account for 73.3 per cent of those employed. Likewise, manufacturing industries now account for only 22.6 per cent of Britain's **Gross Domestic Product (GDP)**.

Some **economists** see this lack of balance as a problem; others see it as a sign of an advanced economy. This book may help you decide for yourself.

▲ A freighter undergoes a refit in a Cornish dockyard – shipbuilding and fitting was once a major secondary industry; falling demand and cheaper shipyards abroad have reduced British shipbuilding to mainly naval contracts.

THE SHAPING OF INDUSTRY

The first real growth of British industry took place in the sixteenth and seventeenth centuries. The discovery of new trade routes to the East, and the **colonization** of North America, opened up new opportunities for the export and trading of British goods. At the same time, people began to recognize the benefits of investing in the expanding industries, such as mining and textiles. Shipbuilding and the building of houses also expanded rapidly to supply Britain's powerful navy and its rapidly growing population. The coal industry also grew to meet the needs of the new blast furnaces used for making iron.

Gradually industry adapted and updated. James Watt's steam-driven engine replaced water, providing a reliable and year-round source of power. The rapid expansion of Britain's roads and canals allowed easier transportation of products to take place.

In 1700, Britain was still a largely farming or agricultural nation, whose people lived in rural areas. By 1831, only 25 per cent of the population were still farming to make their living, and half of the population lived in towns. Britain was going through an **Industrial Revolution**.

▲ Although originally invented by Newcomen to pump water from mines, James Watt improved the efficiency of the steam engine. He invented gears which changed the up and down motion of the beam into a rotating motion that could operate machines.

Until the late 1700s, imported cotton was expensive and spinning and weaving were slow and hard work. Then North America began to grow and harvest cheap cotton, using slave labour. At the same time, a series of inventions, like the flying shuttle and spinning jenny, changed the cotton industry from a process involving a large number of workers to a highly mechanized, steam-powered process. The cotton industry moved from people working in their own houses to factories or mills in Lancashire, Derbyshire and Clydeside. The wool industry soon followed, becoming established around the coal-rich regions of West Yorkshire.

In 1769, Josiah Wedgewood created the first pottery factory near Burslem in Staffordshire. Wedgewood developed the idea of different workers being responsible for different stages in the making of pots. So Wedgewood not only founded the Staffordshire Potteries, but also introduced ideas used in the factory production lines of the twentieth century.

The Industrial Revolution brought many benefits. But increased **mechanization** meant fewer workers. By the early nineteenth century, unemployment and low wages were causing much suffering and unrest. In factories, hours were long, lighting and ventilation bad, and noise levels deafening. Child labour was common and injury from unguarded machinery normal. Epidemics such as cholera and typhoid spread rapidly in the growing towns. Tuberculosis, a lung disease, meant that few workers lived beyond the age of 45 years. Meanwhile the coal-driven machinery belched out black smoke and fumes that darkened the sky and poisoned the land.

▲ 'In the houses one seldom sees a wooded or stone floor, while the doors and windows are nearly always broken and badly fitting. And as for the dirt! Everywhere one sees heaps of refuse, garbage and filth. There are stagnant pools instead of gutters and the stench alone is so overpowering that no human being would find it bearable to live in such a district.' (Merchant visiting Manchester, 1840)

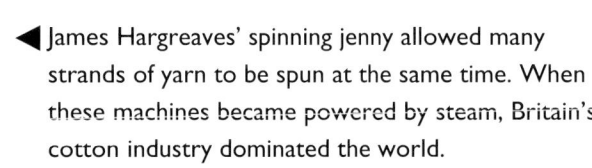

◄ James Hargreaves' spinning jenny allowed many strands of yarn to be spun at the same time. When these machines became powered by steam, Britain's cotton industry dominated the world.

QUARRYING

Industry depends on raw materials or primary commodities such as metals, fibres, coal or petroleum that are used for construction, manufacturing, or the production of energy. One of the most important of these is rock and stone.

Quarrying is a major industry – over £3 billion of aggregates (sand, gravel and crushed rock) are produced each year. Britain has over 1,600 quarries which employ about 32,000 people. In central and south-east England chalk, clay, sand and gravel are quarried for building materials such as bricks and concrete. In the north and west the rocks are harder. Granite and limestone rock are quarried to be used for building roads, while slate is used for roofing.

To reduce both costs and **environmental impact**, quarried materials transported over long distances are sometimes moved by train. A single train can transport 3,000 tonnes – the equivalent of 150 lorry loads!

Quarried materials are not only used in construction. Crushed rock is used in paints, paper, cosmetics and pharmaceuticals, including toothpaste and talcum powder. Sand is used to purify water. Other materials are used in the chemical industry, in agriculture and in the production of glass and steel.

▲ Railway wagons or trucks carrying quarried stone. Over 90 per cent of stone and building material is still transported by road.

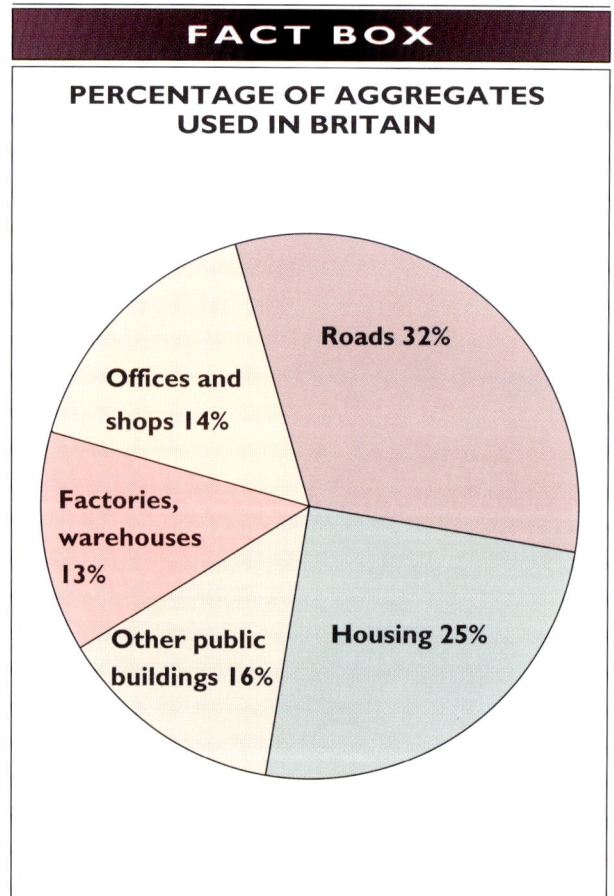

FACT BOX

PERCENTAGE OF AGGREGATES USED IN BRITAIN

Roads 32%
Offices and shops 14%
Factories, warehouses 13%
Other public buildings 16%
Housing 25%

COUNTING THE COST

Quarries are often situated in rural areas where they may damage landscape or local wildlife habitats. Noise, dust and vibration can disrupt nearby communities. Transport by heavy lorries away from the site can cause further disruption.

All quarries must have a restoration plan agreed before work can go ahead. They may be restored as farmland or building sites, or flooded or landscaped to form recreational and conservation areas. They may also be used as landfill sites for the disposal of waste products and rubbish. However, it is essential that there are strict controls to prevent the leakage of poisonous materials into the water system.

Machen quarry near Newport, South Wales, produces a range of construction materials. The company wished to extend the quarry so that it could be worked for another 20 years and the local council agreed to the plan because:

- local jobs would be protected;
- the materials were needed locally;
- the extension would not generate additional traffic;
- an acceptable restoration plan, which stated that the quarry floor would eventually be restored to farmland, was submitted. What other factors might you have considered if you were making this decision?

▲ Rosehill Quarry, Swansea, South Wales. This quarry has been planted over and is now used for recreation.

COAL

In 1750, the amount of coal being mined was about five million tonnes a year. But the demand from the new industries was huge. By 1830, production was 22 million tonnes. In 1914, there were a million coal miners, more than in any other industry except farming. Two hundred and seventy-eight million tonnes of coal were produced from over 3,000 mines.

Until 1947, mines were privately owned. **Industrial relations** were poor because

▲ This mechanical shovel can remove 40 tonnes of earth with each bite. It is used in open-cast mining where the coal is close to the surface.

miners distrusted the owners who were mainly concerned with profit rather than safety. Disputes and strikes were common. To safeguard supplies, coal became the first industry to be nationalized. Under the new National Coal Board (NCB, later to become British Coal) rapid mechanization took place, and safety standards and production rose dramatically.

However, new fuels, particularly oil and natural gas, were becoming available. Gas from coal was, therefore, no longer required and trains were no longer steam-powered.

Cheaper, imported coal came on the market, and the NCB began to close pits. Entire mining communities, particularly those in

South Wales, such as the Rhondda Valley, lost their only source of employment. By 1970, only 293 pits remained open. In 1992, there were less than 50 pits, producing 70 million tonnes with a workforce of 50,000. At the end of 1993, after further closures, the remaining state-owned mines were offered for sale to the private sector. The majority of mines in England are now owned by RJB Mining. The remaining Scottish and Welsh mines are operated by two groups of companies. In addition, there are a number of single, independently owned mines.

Now, fewer than 10,000 miners produce 30 million tonnes of coal a year from deep mines and another 13 million tonnes from open-cast mines. There is plenty of coal left in the ground – perhaps enough to last several hundred years – and coal still provides 25 per cent of all Britain's energy needs. More efficient methods of burning mean that it is still an important fuel for industry, particularly steel.

Coal itself is a versatile product, capable of producing liquid and gas fuels, synthetic fibres and other materials. New technologies are being developed. For example, special techniques allow coal to be burned at very high temperatures with very little production of the compounds that make acid rain.

Many people believe that coal has an important future, while others believe it should be replaced by more modern fuels.

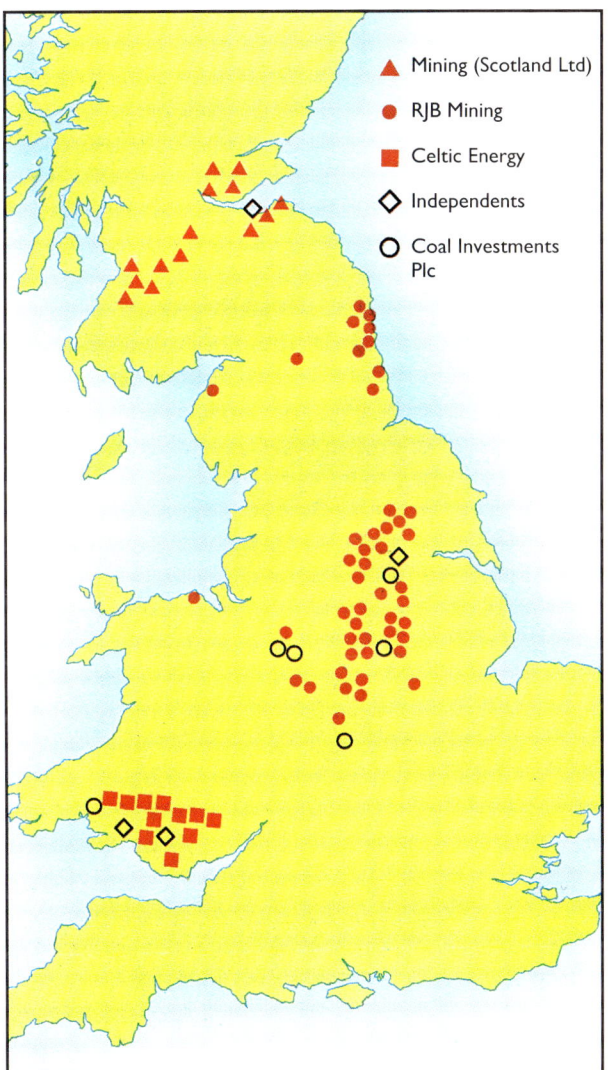

Legend:
- ▲ Mining (Scotland Ltd)
- ● RJB Mining
- ■ Celtic Energy
- ◇ Independents
- ○ Coal Investments Plc

▲ Ownership of coal mines after privatization; in 1914, there were over 3,000 mines in Britain.

OIL AND GAS

Oil forms the basis of much of Britain's industry, both as a source of energy and as a raw material for much of the chemical industry (see pages 20–21). Natural gas is now Britain's most important fuel for household use, and is increasingly used in power stations (see pages 14–15).

Oil was first discovered in Derbyshire in 1847. The following year, James Young set up Britain's first oil refinery. Relatively small amounts of oil were produced from land-based sources, particularly in the South of England, but in the late 1950s and 1960s vast deposits of oil and natural gas were discovered in the North Sea and North Atlantic Ocean.

Oil and gas are usually found, together or separately, in porous reservoir rocks such as sandstone, between shale (oil-bearing rock) and a cap rock (usually clay). They are detected by surveys which build up a picture of the underlying rock formation. Once discovered, movable drilling rigs begin to explore the area. If a reserve is found which is worth extracting, permanent platforms are then installed and production begins. Some platforms are huge and have to withstand some of the most extreme weather conditions in the world. The Ninian Central platform, 160 kilometres off the Shetland Islands, measures 260 metres from top to bottom (twice as high as St Paul's Cathedral) and weighs 620,000 tonnes.

Britain's oil production reached a peak in 1985, rising to 130 million tonnes and earning government income of £3.2 billion. Since then, as reserves have declined and

◀ An oil rig in the North Sea. The larger of the two structures is the service platform where the oil workers live and from which the oil is piped ashore. The raised flat areas are helicopter landing pads.

development of deeper and more remote oil fields becomes more costly, production has dropped to below 90 million tonnes and will continue to do so. Gas production remains high, however, because the demand for it is steadily increasing.

Oil and gas are non-renewable resources which means that they cannot be replaced once used. Estimates of how much oil remains beneath the North Sea vary from 10 to 40 years' supply. Gas estimates vary between 25 to 100 years' supply. There are high environmental costs associated with the extraction, transport, refining and final consumption of these natural resources. The disposal of oil platforms is also expensive and has led to much controversy about whether it is environmentally and economically better for some to be sunk or for them to be taken apart on shore.

▼ This diagram shows a typical cross-section of land where oil and gas are most likely to be found.

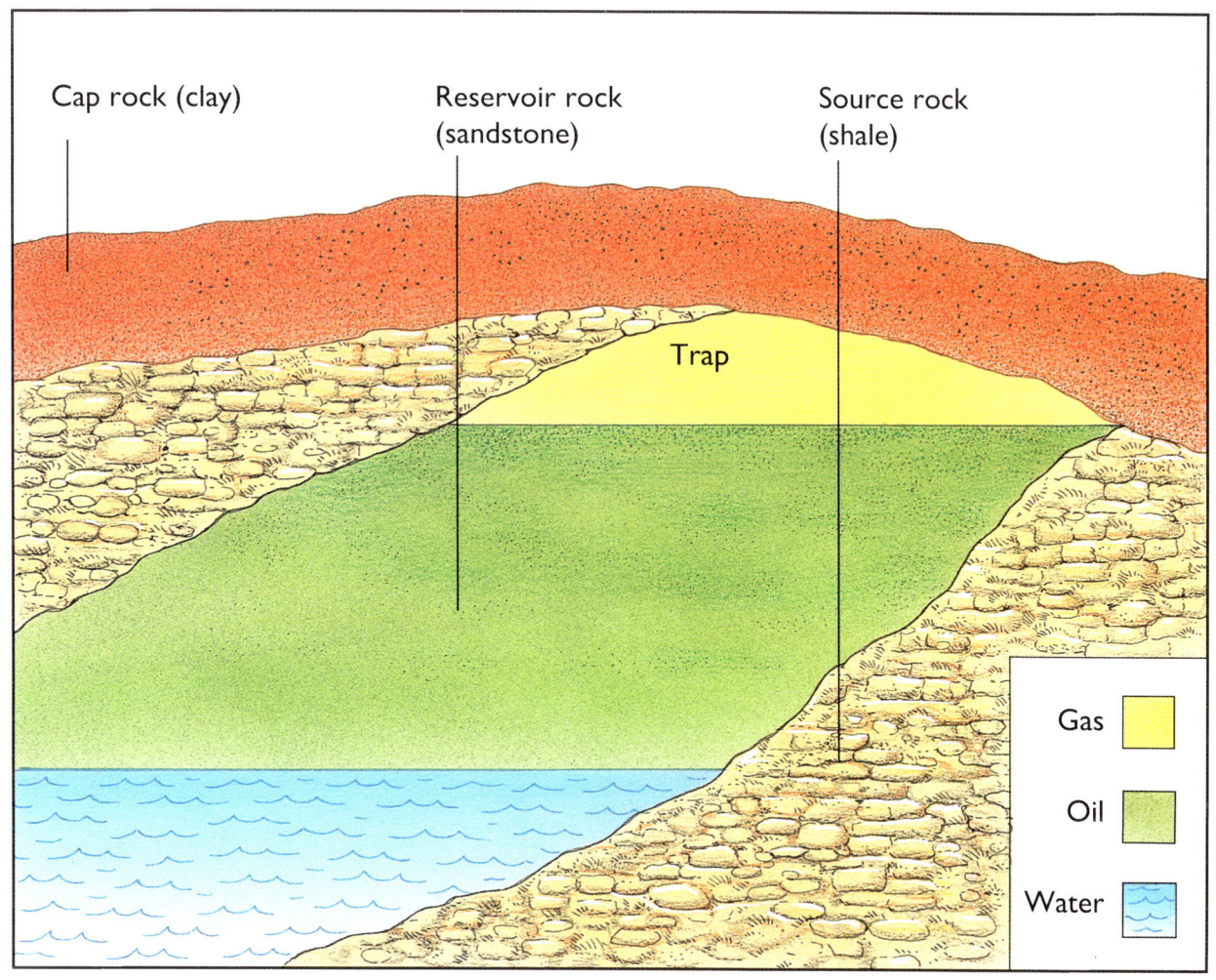

Cap rock (clay)

Reservoir rock (sandstone)

Source rock (shale)

Trap

Gas

Oil

Water

ENERGY

Industry could not exist without energy. Energy powers machinery, heats and lights homes, offices and factories, and runs computers. Britain produces slightly more energy than it uses, mainly because of the large reserves of oil and gas in the North Sea.

FACT BOX

MAIN SOURCES OF ENERGY PRODUCTION IN BRITAIN

☐ Oil (petroleum)	34%
☐ Solid fuels (coal, coke, etc)	27%
☐ Natural gas	27%
☐ Nuclear and hydroelectric	11%
☐ Other (mainly wind)	1%

▲ A nuclear power station – the main emissions in the picture are not polluting gases but steam from the cooling towers. However, concern about the storage and disposal of nuclear waste has hampered the nuclear power industry.

A large proportion of **primary energy sources** such as oil and gas are converted into electricity in power stations. Over 60 per cent of Britain's electricity is produced by coal-burning power stations, 17 per cent is obtained from nuclear power stations, 7 per cent from oil and gas-fired stations and 9 per cent from **hydroelectricity**. There is a move away from coal and oil-burning power stations to gas-fired power stations which produce fewer polluting gases (see pages 42–43). Nuclear power remains an important source of electricity, but public concerns about safety, the problems associated with the disposal of **nuclear waste,** and high costs have halted the expansion of the nuclear industry.

The need to find renewable and less polluting sources of energy has encouraged the development of wind and solar power. Britain has about 20 'wind farms' with a total of 400 wind **turbines**. Development has been limited by difficulties in finding suitable sites and objections to the appearance and sound of large numbers of turbines. Future wind energy sites are therefore likely to be at sea. Tidal and wave power have great potential but are still largely at the experimental stage in Britain.

In recent years, much of Britain's energy production has moved from the public to the private sector. British Gas was privatized in 1986 and competition with other gas supply companies will be allowed in 1996. In 1990, the Central Electricity Generating Board (CEGB) was broken up into three generating (producing) companies and one distribution company. In Scotland, three new companies were formed. In addition, 12 new regional supply companies were formed.

The biggest single user of energy is the iron and steel industry, followed in order by other metal industries, the chemical industry, the glass, pottery and building industries, mining and ore extraction, food and tobacco, textiles, paper and engineering.

In recent years, industry has become more aware of the benefits of **conserving** energy and has now become the most efficient user of energy in Britain.

FACT BOX

MAIN CONSUMERS OF ENERGY IN BRITAIN

Agriculture	0.9%
Iron and steel industry	4.8%
Other industries	20.3%
Railways	0.8%
Road transport	25.1%
Water transport	25.1%
Air transport	4.5%
Domestic use (housing, etc)	25.1%
Public administration (offices, etc)	5.3%
Other	7.4%

MANUFACTURING

Manufacturing firms exist to manufacture or make a product. The **value added** during the production process enables them to sell the finished product at a much higher price than the cost of the raw materials. Although Britain's manufacturing base has declined in recent decades, manufacturing is still a vital part of the nation's economy, employing nearly 6 million people.

PERCENTAGE OF MANUFACTURING WORKFORCE EMPLOYED IN DIFFERENT SECTORS IN BRITAIN

Sector	Percentage
Metals and engineering industries	29%
Food processing	10%
Vehicle manufacture	10%
Paper, printing and publishing	8%
Textiles	6%
Chemical industry	5%

◀ Part of London Docklands undergoing redevelopment. It is hoped that areas like this will generate new industry and increase economic activity.

FACT BOX

FACTORS INFLUENCING THE LOCATION AND TYPE OF MANUFACTURING:

- raw materials – includes minerals such as coal but, more commonly, parts produced by other firms. The location of raw materials is important when they are bulky (for example, brick clay) or spoil rapidly (for example, fruit);

- power – now less important because of easy distribution; some industries which use a great deal of energy, such as aluminium smelting, may be located near sources of cheaper hydroelectricity, as in Scotland;

- markets – nearness to where the product will be sold is important for bulky or perishable goods, such as bread;

- transport – for instance, access to good communication networks (road, rail or waterways) where parts can be assembled and finished products distributed easily;

- labour – important in labour-intensive industries such as clothing manufacture or where highly skilled labour is required. The reliability of the workforce has been an important factor in foreign firms setting up plants in Britain, such as Sony;

- site features – where plants require large areas of inexpensive, flat land, such as car works, oil refineries etc, or a particular commodity, for instance, water for cooling;

- government support – government subsidies and grants, and regional policies have helped industries to move away from the more wealthy South of England, or where traditional employment such as mining has declined.

In the long run an economy that has lost its manufacturing base has lost its vital centre. When manufacturing prospers, all industries connected with it prosper.

Akio Morita, Chairman of Sony

Areas in which Britain has a strong competitive advantage include consumer-packaged goods such as alcoholic drinks, food and household products. Other important areas are petroleum products and chemicals (including paint) pharmaceuticals, household furnishing, computing equipment and software, entertainment and leisure products, office products, defence equipment, motors and engines, and textiles.

The main centres of industry still reflect the distribution of coal fields – particularly in the North of England and Scotland, the West Midlands and the major ports, such as London.

IRON AND STEEL

A modern British steelworks. The success of the industry is very dependent on the state of its main customers such as the car, construction and engineering industries.

Much of British industry was literally built on iron and steel, but the Victorian 'steel masters' who owned the steelworks refused to change and modernize.

Different processes such as iron- and steel-making and rolling (forming the metal into sheets and bars) remained separate, rather than combined. Steelworks were often located where local iron ore or coal was exhausted. Mechanization was slow and working conditions dangerous.

After the Second World War, the industry was nationalized and then reprivatized several times. But, even though production and efficiency increased, the industry could still not reorganize and plan long term. Even so, demand for steel sheet for cars, refrigerators and tin cans increased; huge modern plants were built. Llanwern's strip mill in South Wales could produce up to 50 kilometres of steel strip an hour. But demand began to fall again; poor industrial relations and more cheaply produced steel from Japan and the USA hit the industry. During the 1970s and 1980s, many plants were closed.

The steel industry was reprivatized in 1989 as British Steel Plc which now produces much of Britain's steel plate, track products, tubes and pipes. Another 70 companies produce more specialist goods. Although the steel industry is much smaller, it is now relatively healthy and is expanding slowly. Exports, particularly to the rest of Europe, rose by 7 per cent in 1994.

FACT BOX

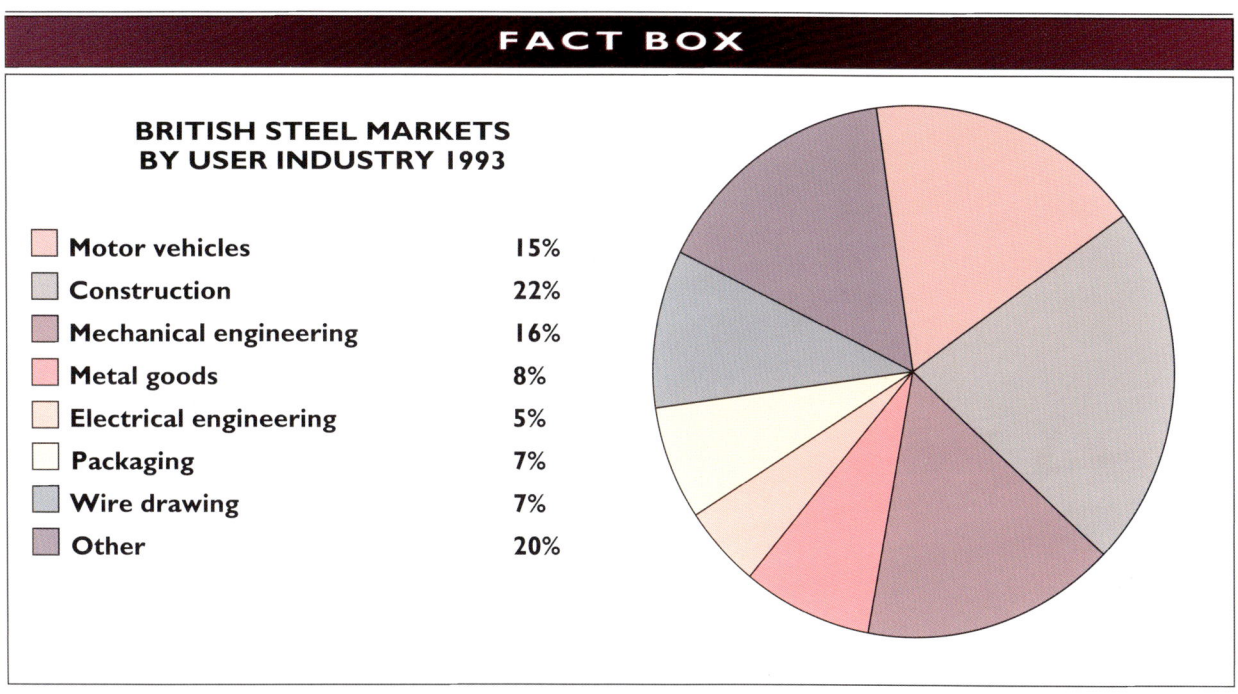

BRITISH STEEL MARKETS BY USER INDUSTRY 1993

	Motor vehicles	15%
	Construction	22%
	Mechanical engineering	16%
	Metal goods	8%
	Electrical engineering	5%
	Packaging	7%
	Wire drawing	7%
	Other	20%

CASE STUDY

SCUNTHORPE WORKS

Scunthorpe is one of British Steel's four combined steel plants with a capacity of four million tonnes of steel a year and a workforce of approximately 4,000.

Molten iron is produced by feeding a mixture of coke, iron oxide (ore) and limestone into the blast furnace, where a blast of hot air causes the mixture to burn at white heat. The coke (carbon) produces carbon monoxide which reacts with iron oxide, producing molten iron and carbon dioxide. Limestone removes any impurities.

The molten iron is tapped off and loaded into a basic oxygen converter with about 25 per cent scrap steel. Oxygen is blown through at high speed and the newly formed steel runs off into moulds or is rolled into sheets. Sophisticated computer software allows temperature and other operations to be monitored constantly.

Steel from Scunthorpe has been used in the construction of the Humber Bridge, the Channel Tunnel (40,000 tonnes), Canary Wharf and coat hangers!

CHEMICALS

The chemical industry arose in the eighteenth and nineteenth centuries from the need for practical materials such as bleaching agents for textiles, soap, glass, agricultural chemicals, explosives and chemicals used for making paper.

At the turn of the twentieth century, Britain's chemical industry was in decline. The First World War saw its recovery as Britain became more self-sufficient in drugs, dyes and explosives. Between the two wars, some of the major chemical companies such as ICI and Unilever were formed, mainly through mergers of smaller firms. This period also saw the development of the modern synthetic fibre industry, plastics and resins, and pharmaceuticals. The petrochemical industry expanded rapidly, based on products formed as a result of oil refining. During and after the Second World War the **agrochemical** industry grew enormously in order to increase food production. More recently the need for ultra-pure elements for the electronics industry such as silicon, has stimulated further growth.

▲ A chemical plant producing carbonic acid at the turn of the century. Today there are over 60,000 manufactured chemicals in everyday use. The effect of many of them on humans and the environment is not fully understood.

Today, Britain's chemical industry is the fifth largest in the world after the USA, Japan, Germany and France, with a workforce of 300,000, a **turnover** of £32 billion and net exports (exports less imports) of £3.8 billion. It is based traditionally in the north-west and north-east of England and Yorkshire. The expansion of petrochemicals has also encouraged development in South Wales, Southampton and Scotland.

Apart from the chemical industry itself, the main industries it supplies include agriculture, electronics, power, motor vehicles, aerospace, healthcare and cosmetics, food manufacture and construction. Future emphasis is likely to be on the development of so-called advanced materials (for example, ceramics and fabrics) to meet specific and demanding situations, such as in aerospace.

Modern chemicals have improved many aspects of people's lives, for example, in relation to health and food production. But many have also caused great harm. Organic pesticides such as DDT and Dieldrin are now banned, because of their long-term effects on wildlife and humans. **CFCs (chlorofluorocarbons),** used in the electronics industry and as coolants, are partly responsible for the erosion of the ozone layer. The chemical industry now has an important role to play – the development of non-polluting production methods will mean less use of toxic products.

FACT BOX

SECTORS OF THE CHEMICAL INDUSTRY 1991

Pharmaceuticals	35%
Soap and toilet preparation	10%
Organics	12%
Inorganics	4%
Fertilizers	2%
Specialized chemical products	3%
Industrial/agricultural use	9%
Paints, varnishes and printing inks	6%
Dyestuffs and printing inks	3%
Plastics, synthetic resins/rubbers	6%
Other	10%

ENGINEERING

E ngineering has existed since the invention of the wheel. The Egyptians and Greeks were talented engineers 2,000–3,000 years ago (think of the pyramids!) and Leonardo da Vinci was designing helicopters in the fourteenth century. Engineering really became established, however, during the Industrial Revolution. Brilliant engineers such as James Watt, who perfected the steam engine, and Isambard Brunel who designed ships, tunnels and bridges of great imagination and scale, transformed the face of Britain. More recently, engineering has evolved into different branches such as **civil engineering,** chemical engineering, electrical and electronic engineering, aerospace and mechanical engineering.

▲ Isambard Kingdom Brunel is best known for building bridges and railways, including Paddington Station in London. His greatest work, however, was the construction of iron steamships powered by propellers rather than paddlewheels.

FACT BOX

ENGINEERING EXPORTS, IMPORTS AND EMPLOYMENT IN BRITAIN (1994)

	EXPORTS (£billion)	IMPORTS (£billion)	EMPLOYMENT (thousands)
Electrical and instrument engineering	30.28	31.8	581
Mechanical engineering	13.19	10.81	527
Metal goods	2.52	2.76	314
Motor vehicles	10.45	16.81	214
Other transport equipment	7.24	6.15	191

CASE STUDY

MAGNETS BEAT X-RAY

A firm in **Oxford** produces electromagnets for use in body-imaging machines. These machines produce images rather like X-rays but are based on minute magnetic fields given off by body tissues. The company produces **300 electromagnets a year** which are sold to companies who make the machines themselves. A single electro-magnet sells for nearly a quarter of a million pounds!

The main expense is in the wire used in the coils of the magnet which has to carry very high electric currents without heating up. The winding of the wire needs to be so accurate that this is done by computers. The coiled electromagnet is then placed in a liquid gas at -269°C. The whole operation is carried out by four highly skilled engineers, each entirely responsible for one stage in the production process.

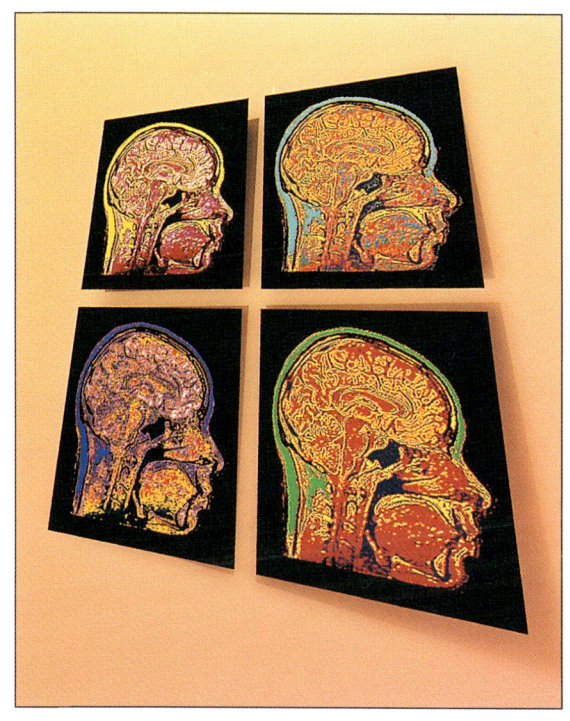

▲ Electromagnetic images of the brain. These scans have been produced by 'magnetic resonance imaging' and can provide more detail than X-rays.

Engineering is a highly skilled activity covering a wide range of manufacturing. Most engineering companies are small and medium-sized enterprises (SMEs) with less than 150 employees. Total employment in the engineering industry is about 1.84 million.

Like many other industries, British engineering was hit by the **recession** in the early 1990s. Since that time, however, it has begun to recover. The most rapid expansion has been in telecommunications and computer equipment and in motor vehicles and their parts.

Employment in engineering has fallen steadily in recent years. The emphasis on highly skilled technical expertise has resulted in a serious shortage of skilled workers in some parts of the industry.

MOTOR VEHICLES

The founder of Britain's motor industry could be said to be William Morris. He followed the ideas of factory-produced cars that Henry Ford had developed so successfully in the USA with his famous 'Model T'. By 1925, Morris was producing 52,000 cars a year – half of Britain's car output – with a workforce of 14,000.

Britain continued to be a leading car manufacturer between the First and Second World Wars. But, by the 1950s and 1960s, outdated management, lack of **investment** in new technology, and boring work on the assembly lines, led to poor industrial relations and low productivity. By the early 1970s, 40 per cent of all British cars were imported with the greatest competition coming from Europe and Japan. Britain's motor industry was reduced to four main manufacturers – British Leyland (BL), Ford, Vauxhall and Chrysler. Of these, only BL was not owned by the USA, and only Ford was making a profit.

▲ The famous Ford Model T manufactured in the USA by Henry Ford in 1915. Ford pioneered the idea of assembly (production) lines which dominated industry for over half a century.

FACT BOX

COMPARISON OF VEHICLE PRODUCTION IN BRITAIN BETWEEN 1981 AND 1991

	1981	1991
Passenger car (total)	954,650	1,236,900
1000 cc and under	229,189	26,621
1000–1600 cc	526,498	830,530
1600–2800 cc	153,957	338,877
Over 2800 cc	45,006	40,872
Commercial vehicles (total)	225,634	214,441
Vans	157,744	184,005
Trucks:		
Under 7.5 tonnes	14,294	8,833
Over 7.5 tonnes	41,152	11,766
Buses, coaches and minibuses:		
Single deck	9,903	9,426
Double deck	2,541	411

British Leyland was nationalized in the mid-1970s and made more efficient. But this also meant the loss of thousands of jobs.

Automation had been introduced onto the assembly (production) line in the early 1950s. Computer-controlled welding robots followed in the 1970s and computerized machining of engine parts was introduced in the late 1980s. BL was sold off, the most successful part of the company becoming the Rover Group, now owned by BMW.

In recent years, the motor industry in Britain has been more successful, although there are now no major British-owned companies in operation. Japanese firms, such as Toyota, Nissan and Honda, now have major plants in Britain. British firms, however, are still noted for luxury cars and sports cars.

CASE STUDY

RESEARCHING ALTERNATIVES TO PETROL

The development of cars with improved safety, economy and environmental performance has been a feature of car production in the 1990s. Despite this, exhaust emissions from vehicles continue to rise as the number and use of cars increases (see pages 38–39).

Ford are currently developing an electric vehicle based on the Ford Escort. It can cover over 100 miles (160 kilometres) and carry over half a tonne in weight. Performance is increased by lightweight materials, a braking system that returns energy to the battery, and low resistance tyres. Ford is also working on vehicles powered by hydrocarbons such as methanol, which give off carbon dioxide but no other pollutants.

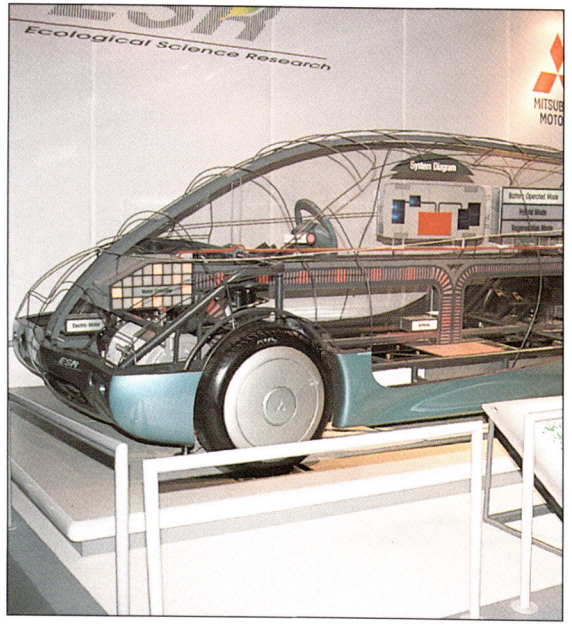

▲ The car of the future? This vehicle, designed by Mitsubishi, can run on either electricity or petrol. What other features will improve its environmental performance?

ELECTRONICS

◀ A British electronics factory. The working conditions in modern electronic plants are controlled very exactly, so that dust and other damaging particles are kept out of the workplace.

Electronics is forecast to be the world's largest single industry by the year 2000. It covers telecommunications, computer technology and software, defence equipment, electrical manufacturing and business equipment. The electronics industry is the key technology for almost every other area of industry.

The foundations for the modern electronics industry were laid during the Second World War with the development of radar, navigation systems and machines for decoding messages. This was soon followed by television. Bulky valves were replaced by smaller parts, but defence and space programmes required further miniaturization. A British scientist first put forward the idea of an electrical circuit made from a single piece of silicon (microchip), but Britain rapidly lost ground to the USA and Japan. British expertise developed the pocket calculator, the digital watch and the home computer, but lack of support again lost Britain the advantage.

Although Japan and the USA still dominate the industry, Britain has again achieved a world position in electronics, particularly in relation to aerospace (see pages 28–29), defence and telecommunications. Japanese electronics firms such as Sony and Toshiba have set up plants in Britain, particularly Scotland. Other companies have moved parts of their production outside Britain, where labour costs are lower.

Exports now account for 44 per cent of total sales, with the most rapid growth being in the radio communications (for example, cellular phones), personal computer and data communication markets.

The future of the electronics industry is likely to be in the fields of communication networks and multimedia technology.

FACT BOX

SALES AND EXPORTS OF ELECTRONIC EQUIPMENT (£BILLION)

	Britain	Export	Total
Data processing equipment	4,581	4,693	9,274
Electronic parts	2,246	980	3,226
Office machinery	218	165	383
Radio and electrical goods	2,704	2,049	4,753
Telecommunications	1,563	911	2,474
Total electronics industry	**11,312**	**8,798**	**20,110**

CASE STUDY

VIRTUAL REALITY

The Leicester-based virtual reality (VR) system developer **Virtuality Group** and **Atari** are producing the first total VR games system for the consumer market. Virtuality are developing the prototype consumer head mounted display (HMD) for Atari's 64-bit Jaguar system. Atari are contributing to the development costs.

Full-scale production of the HMDs began in 1995 at a price of around $200 (£120).

▲ As well as developing interactive, three-dimensional games, virtual reality has important applications in training pilots and others where complex and demanding situations need to be artificially created.

AEROSPACE

At the height of the Second World War, aircraft building was the biggest industry in the country, employing 1,700,000 people. Aeroplanes like the Lancaster, Spitfire and Hurricane became household names. Soon after the War, the Vickers Viscount became the most successful British airliner ever made. The first jet airliner, the Comet, was three years ahead of its American rivals when a series of tragic crashes set back the industry. Gradually the American giants Boeing and Douglas overtook the British passenger aircraft industry. The development of the Anglo-French supersonic Concorde during the 1970s was a triumph of engineering and design, but sharply rising fuel prices and its high noise level made it an economic disaster.

▲ A Hawker Hurricane flies over the countryside of south-east England. The Hurricane was the most successful British fighter 'plane of the Second World War. It had a top speed of 483 kph and could be flown from aircraft carriers and specially equipped merchant ships.

◀ A Sea Harrier leaves its carrier. The Harrier revolutionized fighter aircraft design by being able to take off vertically using rotating engine nozzles. This allows the 'plane to operate from unprepared or limited landing areas.

CASE STUDY

BRITISH AEROSPACE

British Aerospace (BA) has a current workforce of 45,000. Its major activity is in the development of defence systems such as Tornadoes, training aircraft, missiles and navigation systems. BA is a partner in the Eurofighter 2000 project and part of a French / German / British partnership producing the Tiger 'Eurocopter'. BA also produces naval craft and weapons fired from the ground. Eighty-two per cent of BA's £7 billion defence orders are exports.

BA is also a commercial aerospace company with £4.2 billion of orders. It is a partner, with France, Germany and Spain, in the successful Airbus Industrie, producing wide-bodied and 'regular' transport and passenger aircraft powered by Rolls Royce engines. BA is also involved, with Aerospaciale of France and Alenia of Italy, in the production of smaller aircraft

designed for shorter flights. This partnership recently secured a deal with the American Trans States Airlines for 60 of its Jetstream aircraft. This will safeguard 2,000 jobs at its Prestwick plant in Scotland.

▲ Engineers winching a jet engine into place at British Aerospace. By involving other European countries in aerospace projects, development and production costs can be shared and larger numbers of aircraft manufactured.

However, Britain continued to produce a series of highly successful military aircraft, including the Hawker Hunter, the Canberra, the Tornado and the Harrier jump jet.

Meanwhile, aircraft manufacturers came together to form larger companies such as the British Aircraft Corporation (BAC) and Hawker Siddeley. They began to concentrate on military projects, helicopters, engines and

missiles. As the space industry grew, BAC expanded to become British Aerospace. The vast development costs of aerospace projects encouraged cooperation with European partners. Britain is a member of the European Space Agency (ESA) which developed the Ariane launch vehicle as a competitor to the American Space Shuttle, and SPACELAB, a laboratory module carried by the shuttle.

CONSTRUCTION

The construction industry is central to the British economy, employing nearly one million people on projects ranging from the Channel Tunnel, airports, railways, hospitals, offices, motorways, harbours and shopping malls to housing extensions.

Building in progress at ▶ Canary Wharf, London Docklands. The Docklands light railway and the City of London can be seen in the background.

◀ A construction site begins to take shape. Any major construction project will involve a number of stages and many different professionals including planners, estimators, architects, surveyors, engineers and construction managers.

Traditionally the focus of the construction industry has been large-scale engineering projects such as motorways and factories. There is now a growing shift towards the renovation and restoration of existing sites, for example, the regeneration of London and Liverpool docklands. Construction companies are privately owned in Britain; the majority are small with less than 50 employees; a few are giants such as Tarmac, Wimpey and Trafalgar House which employ thousands of people.

FACT BOX

MAJOR TYPES OF CONSTRUCTION IN BRITAIN

Upkeep and improvement of existing buildings	25%
New housing	40%
Construction of transport network and civil engineering	15%
Non-residential public buildings (council buildings, etc)	5%
Non-residential private buildings (offices, etc)	15%

Recent laws and greater awareness of the need to take into account the environmental impact of projects, have encouraged the development of environmental engineering. Before major projects begin, an assessment is carried out to look at the likely effect the development will have and how any potentially damaging effects can be reduced. Even so, decisions may not always satisfy all the different groups concerned, for example, where a bypass is involved. The construction process itself often involves the use of heavy machinery, large amounts of energy (fuel) and extraction of raw materials which may harm the environment.

CASE STUDY

MANCHESTER AIRPORT

In the late 1980s, Manchester Airport was faced with an increase in passengers and a terminal which was unable to cope with further expansion. A two-phase project was designed to increase capacity by 1993 and to allow further expansion which would support 24 million passengers by 1998 at a total cost of £0.5 billion.

A study was carried out to look at the possibility of building a second terminal. The study looked at its layout, passenger management and type of air traffic. A T-shaped building was designed with a central terminal complex and a pier facing the aircraft holding areas. The terminal was designed to minimize walking distances and to cater for elderly or disabled passengers and children. Shops and cafés, 55 check-in desks and five 70-metre baggage reclaim units were also included. Motorway interchange, parking and hotel facilities were also taken into consideration.

The need for flexibility of use, difficult ground conditions, and tight schedules were all built into the planning of the overall project. The project was completed on schedule, designed for both present and future use as a new addition to a major international airport.

TEXTILES

Textiles could be said to be Britain's oldest industry. In 1912, the cotton industry alone supported a workforce of 600,000, whose skill could not be matched anywhere else in the world. Much of the industry was based in Lancashire. It had two-thirds of world trade and cotton goods made up a quarter of British exports.

Like many other British industries, however, the cotton textile industry was slow to change and adapt to new markets and technology. New industries developed in Europe, South America, China, Japan and India. Often they were more efficient and labour was cheaper. British clothing manufacturers began importing yarn and cloth from abroad. A modern weaving mill, opened by Courtaulds in the mid-1960s in Skelmersdale, Lancashire, was closed within eight years.

The development of synthetic fibres from petrochemicals did much to revolutionize the industry. Polyester fibres were developed by ICI in the 1940s and acrylics developed by Courtaulds in 1957. These fibres last longer, are very strong, are less likely to stain and do not crease. Often they are combined with natural fibres to produce garments that are easy to look after. More recently, microfibres and super-microfibres have been developed to give fabrics finer textures.

FACT BOX		
IMPORTS AND EXPORTS OF TEXTILES AND CLOTHING (£ MILLION)		
	Imports	Exports
TEXTILES		
Fibres		
Synthetic fibres	248	242
Wool	39	92
Cotton	96	6
Woven fabrics		
Synthetic	478	113
Wool	16	134
Cotton	332	140
Knitted fabrics	63	39
Carpets	117	104
Other (furnishings, etc)	509	418
CLOTHING		
Knitted	1,545	315
Not knitted	1,851	513
Other (leather, etc)	231	49
TOTAL	5,525	2,165

A length of super-microfibre stretching to the moon would only weigh about 42 grams!

Now British textiles is a relatively small, highly technological and successful industry. Computers control machinery and are also used by fabric and clothes designers to create patterns and designs on screen. Britain's sixth largest export industry is woollen textiles, running at about £585 million a year.

British-finished products such as clothes, household furnishings and leather goods also make an important contribution to the economy. Even so, Britain imports far more textiles and finished products than it exports. This is partly because of low wage structures outside Britain and partly because of high import duties charged by some countries to protect their own industries. Britain also supports the Multifibre Arrangement which promotes exports from developing countries.

CASE STUDY

NEW FIBRES

In June 1995, Courtaulds, the chemical giant, announced a new technical breakthrough in the production of **TENCEL**, the company's new spun fibre made from cellulose. This development has allowed Courtaulds to increase the output of its existing **TENCEL** plants because it means that spinning rates can be greatly increased. The company plans to build a new plant at Grimsby, to incorporate the new technology, with a final capacity of 40,000 tonnes of material a year.

◀ Thoroughly modern denim made from TENCEL. Although the fabric looks just like traditional denim, it has a much softer feel.

FOOD AND DRINK

Britain is among the most advanced food manufacturing and marketing nations in the world. The industry employs 3.6 million people ranging from the people who grow the food such as farmers, to manufacturers and retailers. Production accounts for 9 per cent of gross domestic product (GDP) and means that customers spend £91 billion a year. Even so, Britain imports more food than it exports.

FACT BOX

ANNUAL PRODUCTION OF BRITISH PROCESSED FOODS (THOUSAND TONNES)	
Margarine and other table spreads	475
Solid cooking fats	121
Jam and marmalade	181
Syrup and treacle	51
Canned vegetables	732
Canned and bottled fruit	37
Soups (canned and powdered)	314
Tinned meat	118
Biscuits	724
Breakfast cereals	273
Chocolate confectionery	483
Sugar confectionery	327
Sugar, etc	546
Soft drinks (million litres)	
Concentrated	557
Unconcentrated	4,316

One of the fastest growing sectors in the food industry is catering. Britain has over 125,000 catering establishments (restaurants, public houses, cafés, etc) with a turnover of nearly £30 billion. The catering industry employs 1.25 million people.

Food retailing is changing rapidly. The major change has been from small shops (butchers, bakers, etc) to supermarkets and 'superstores' which sell household and other items as well as food. Sainsbury's, Tesco, Safeway, Argyll and Asda now account for 62 per cent of total retail sales. Another trend has been the growth of shops catering for particular tastes, such as vegetarian shops and delicatessens.

The fresh food section of a supermarket. Most shoppers prefer to select their own goods, but customer demand for perfectly shaped fruit and vegetables can lead to wastage of products.

A health food shop. Greater awareness of the possible dangers of foods produced with the use of artificial chemicals has given rise to a market for organically grown produce.

CASE STUDY

BRITISH SUGAR

British Sugar is part of the Associated British Foods group of companies which produce a wide range of products ranging from bread and biscuits to tea. The company manufactures sugar from sugar beet, grown mainly in the east of England. It has recently completed a £50 million modernization and expansion of its plant at Wissington, making it one of the largest and most modern sugar beet manufacturing units in the world. The plant can handle up to 15,000 tonnes of sugar beet per day.

Like many British firms, British Sugar has moved into other related areas such as seed pelleting, with factories in Norfolk, Ireland and California. It is also involved in the production of animal feeds and has recently joined together the operations of a number of its other animal feed companies, as Associated British Nutrition. Another of its smaller companies, ABR foods, has installed a new glucose refinery at its Corby site, producing a range of glucose syrups for sale to the confectionery industry.

British Sugar has an active research and development programme, developing a range of new food ingredients at a new site in Telford.

SERVICING INDUSTRY

Service industries play an important part in generating the wealth of an economy. As industry becomes more complex, the need for more sophisticated methods of research, selling, communications, finance (for example, banking, investment and insurance) and management also grows.

This may involve scientists, lawyers, accountants and financial experts, public relations experts, management consultants, market researchers, and sales specialists.

Such specialists may be employed within a company itself, or work for an agency engaged by the company. The majority of small and medium-sized enterprises (SMEs) operate in the service industry sector.

The greatest increase in service industries has been in the so-called market sector, that is activities to do with the distribution and sale (wholesale and retail) of products.

In particular, the supermarket, hotel and restaurant sectors have seen massive expansion in recent years.

There has been an enormous growth in the service industry, but it cannot exist on its own. A healthy economy must therefore seek to keep a balance between what it produces and how that production is serviced.

Customers at a ▶ supermarket checkout. The trend for supermarkets and superstores to be sited outside towns has been halted because it has caused high street shops to lose trade and be closed down.

THE BIG SELL

Levi Strauss are the world's largest manufacturers of jeans. In the early 1980s, however, jeans were becoming less popular with young people who associated them with their parents' generation. In an effort to maintain their place in the market, the company expanded into other areas, producing a range of products bearing the Levi brand name, such as shirts and jackets.

Although successful, the name Levi was seen on too many products. So, the company decided to return to their traditional strengths, relaunching Levi 501s with a massive advertising campaign aimed at young men.

Market research suggested that young people were interested in their past, particularly the USA of the 1950s. Levi's advertising consultants developed a series of advertisements using this theme. In one, a young man removes his Levis in an old-fashioned launderette in order to wash them. In a more recent version, two young women from an obviously sheltered family 'out-west', watch a man emerging from a creek in a pair of shrink-to-fit Levi 501s.

As a result of this marketing plan, Levi Strauss regained their market share.

TRANSPORT

Industry relies on efficient methods of transport to move raw materials and goods (freight) and people to the right locations in Britain and abroad. Transport represents about 5 per cent of Britain's GDP and employs 5 per cent of the workforce. It uses over 30 per cent of Britain's energy requirements and takes up nearly 40 per cent of public money!

Britain has approximately 55 kilometres of rail network per 1,000 square kilometres of land. The networks were run privately until 1948, when they were nationalized and run by British Rail (BR). In 1994, BR ceased to be responsible for the provision of rail services, but continues to operate businesses such as Intercity and Railfreight, as they are sold or **franchised** to the private sector. All passenger services are currently being divided into 25 train-operating units and again franchised to the private sector. The ownership of track, land and stations has been passed to Railtrack, which will also eventually be privatized.

Britain has 18 international airports. British Airways is the main carrier, carrying 25.5 million passengers and 506,000 tonnes of cargo per year. In 1992, British airlines flew 800 million kilometres, enough for nearly three round trips to the sun.

There are about 5,600 kilometres of usable canals and rivers in Britain of which about 616 kilometres are regularly used for cargo.

◀ Waterloo Station in the evening rush hour. Many commuters are still reluctant to use the railways because of factors such as cost, reliability and feelings of personal freedom they associate with driving their own cars.

Britain also has a merchant fleet but most ships are no longer registered in this country for financial reasons. British ports handle over 300 million tonnes of goods each year.

Britain has about 25 kilometres of motorway per 1,000 square kilometres and a total of 387,000 kilometres of roadways. £2.5 billion per year is spent on Britain's roadways.

The transport of goods within Britain is almost all by road. Most agricultural and foodstuffs are transported in this way, as are building materials, chemicals and manufactured articles.

The concerns about the reliance on moving cargo by road are traffic jams and air pollution caused by exhaust emissions from cars and lorries. However, until the railways are in a position to offer a more competitive alternative, or attitudes towards the use of cars changes, this situation is likely to continue.

▲ A commercial truck hauls its 30-tonne load along a British motorway. Many people would like to see a shift of freight to the railways and better links of road and rail networks so that goods can be switched more easily between the two.

FACT BOX

GOODS TRANSPORTED BY ROAD, RAIL AND INLAND WATERWAYS (PER CENT BY WEIGHT)

Product	Road	Rail	Inland waterways
Agricultural products	94	4	2
Foodstuffs	95	2	3
Solid mineral fuels (coal, etc)	45	48	7
Petroleum products	77	8	15
Ore and scrap metal	46	33	21
Metal products	62	32	6
Minerals and building materials	93	2	5
Fertilizers	76	15	9
Chemicals	90	7	3
Manufactured articles	93	6	1

THE WORKFORCE

The most important factor in industry's success is its workforce. Research has shown that successful companies are ones in which employees understand and identify with the aims of the company and whose potential is recognized and channelled in the right direction. Good management and training has a vital role in achieving this.

In the past, working conditions were often poor, hours were long and safety usually ignored. At the beginning of this century, children as young as 12 might work 60 or 70 hours a week. Accidents were frequent. In 1912, there were 3,995 reported deaths due to industry, 1,100 in mines alone. Injury was an accepted part of the working routine. Many deaths went unrecorded because people died away from work. The coal dust

▲ Striking coal miners held a mass demonstration in London in 1984 to protest against the number of pit closures and loss of jobs.

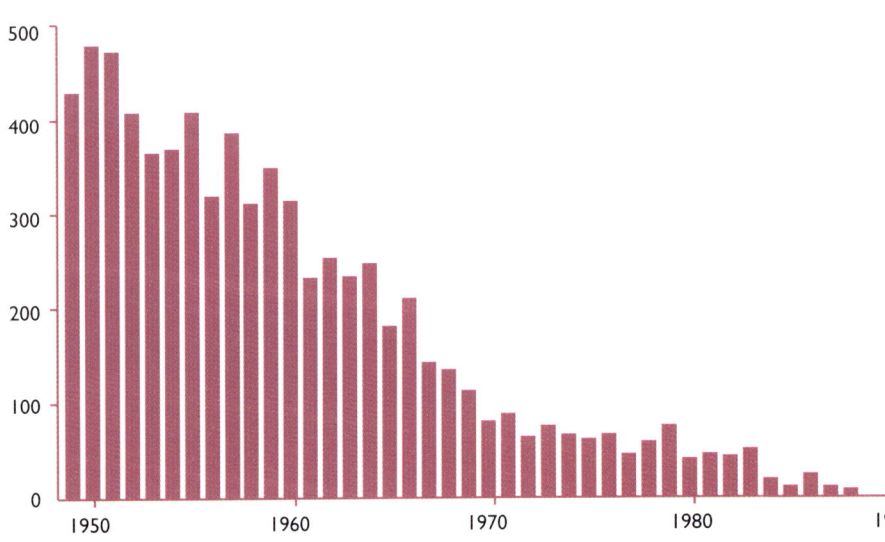

◀ Numbers of fatal accidents in the coal mining industry between 1950 and 1990 in Britain.

in mines, the particles and gases of steel works, and the tiny floating fibres in textile mills, all contributed to early death or crippling lung and skin diseases. Deaths caused by industry today are nearer 500 and most people would still consider this to be too high.

One factor in the improvement of safety has been the influence of trade unions. Unions began at the beginning of the Industrial Revolution as an attempt by workers to improve wages and working conditions. They were often successful, but the fighting approach between employers and unions damaged much of British industry. Now unions have a broader welfare, training and educational role. Working days lost through strikes and other stoppages have decreased by over 80 per cent in the past 10 years.

There are 268 unions in Britain with a membership of nine million – about 35 per cent of the working population.

Training at all levels of industry is very important. This includes better education and training before employment, and training while working. Surprisingly, Britain still has skill shortages in many areas of industry, for example in electronics and engineering. Increasingly, training while working involves attending courses in training schools or colleges. A key aim of training is to allow people to adapt to new situations or technology. It also means they are better equipped to make decisions, at whatever position they hold in the workplace. The days of repetitive and boring factory work are largely gone. Industry now needs a thinking workforce.

A British business ▶
training seminar. The
need to continue to
develop the skills,
flexibility and
knowledge of
employees
throughout their
careers is now
recognized by all
successful industries.

THE ENVIRONMENT

The Industrial Revolution had a devastating effect on the environment. But more modern processes have been equally damaging. Polychlorinated biphenyls (PCBs) were first manufactured in 1928 and became widely used in lubricants, hydraulic systems, cement, adhesives, plastics and plaster. It was not until 1968, that people realized that PCBs were highly toxic to both animals and humans. They are difficult to destroy. Although the use of PCBs has now been largely phased out, millions of litres remain in old machinery, landfill sites and electrical equipment – an environmental time bomb.

The burning of fossil fuels (coal, oil and gas) produce oxides of sulphur and nitrogen which create acid rain and damage health. A number of power stations are now fitted with desulphurization units and all new cars are fitted with catalytic converters, which cut down, but do not eliminate, these products. The burning of these fuels also produces carbon dioxide, which contributes to global warming and cannot be eliminated by filters. Natural gas produces 40 per cent less carbon dioxide than coal, practically no sulphur oxides and fewer nitrogen oxides. It is therefore the cleanest of the fossil fuels. Britain is committed to reducing carbon dioxide emissions to 1990 levels by the year 2000 and to reducing sulphur dioxide by 60

FACT BOX

SULPHUR DIOXIDE EMISSIONS

Power stations	72%
Other industry	19%
Other sectors	4%
Domestic	3%
Road transport	2%

NITROGEN OXIDES EMISSIONS

Road transport	51%
Power stations	28%
Other industry	10%
Other sources	8%
Domestic	2%

CARBON DIOXIDE EMISSIONS

Power stations	34%
Other industry	26%
Road transport	19%
Domestic	14%
Commercial/public services	5%

per cent of 1980 levels by 2003. Many people do not think that these reductions are enough.

Many industries now look at the environmental impact of a product at all stages in its design, use of raw materials, production and use, right through to final disposal or recycling. This process is called life-cycle analysis. Consumers too, are an important part of this process, demanding environmentally friendly products and rejecting others, and so influencing industry.

All types of businesses have an environmental impact; the challenge is for them to identify this impact and take steps to reduce it.

Industry needs to be sustainable; that is to operate in such a way that the earth's resources and its natural systems are not threatened, either now or in the future.

◀ Sustainable industry in action. These beech trees in a Hertfordshire wood are being coppiced, that is, managed to provide timber for fencing and other purposes every 15 or 20 years. They also provide a valuable habitat for wildlife.

THE FUTURE

Throughout the eighteenth and nineteenth centuries, Britain was one of the strongest industrial and trading nations in the world. But Britain's major industries were slow to modernize and change. As other countries became more industrialized, their own manufactured goods replaced British products and then competed with them elsewhere.

Britain attempted to protect its position against cheaper imported goods by imposing complicated trade agreements and taxes. In recent years, however, there has been an attempt to simplify trade regulations and allow a freer flow of goods between countries. There has also been a move to protect countries with developing economies. The General Agreement on Tariffs and Trade (GATT) is a series of agreements designed to encourage this freer flow of goods.

New industrial economies are emerging. The most important of these has been Japan. Other Pacific countries such as South Korea, Malaysia and Singapore, with highly skilled workforces and relatively cheap labour also compete on the world market. Giant nations like China, India and the countries of South America are also industrializing rapidly and provide an increasing amount of competition for British companies.

Like many western countries, Britain has gone through a difficult recession and is emerging with a smaller but more *focused* industrial base. British industry is now highly automated and well managed.

Companies with similar interests cooperate more; some have joined together to form larger units. Further trends have been the rise of small and medium-sized businesses and an increase in part-time work. Many more people are now self-employed or working from a computer at home.

However, despite falling slowly, unemployment remains high and people worry about job security. Shareholders and directors often appear to reap the benefits of success at the expense of the workforce. While women have made many advances in industry, few hold top management positions.

▶ Japan has had a phenomenal growth in industry since the Second World War. Consumer goods, computing, electronics and robotics have all played an important part in Japan's success. Today aerospace and biotechnology are at the forefront of Japanese industry. Japan competes successfully with European and American firms to develop new industries.

Much of Britain's past industrial success was built on taking advantage of people and the world's resources. Today we might wish to question whether it is right or wrong to make and export sophisticated weapons. So, industry in Britain today is about choice. The famous industrialist, Sir John Harvey-Jones, has said that the purpose of industry is to create wealth. We have to recognize the difference between wealth and *cost*, that is, what we are prepared to pay in terms of the environment and the type of society we want to live in, in order to gain the benefits that successful industry can bring.

▶ Anita Roddick. The Body Shop dedicates its business to the pursuit of social and environmental change. It creatively balances the financial and human needs of its employees, customers, franchisees, suppliers and shareholders.

GLOSSARY

Agrochemical
Chemicals made for agriculture, for example, fertilizers and pesticides.

Automation
The introduction of computer-aided and automatic processes, including robots, which increase efficiency, usually resulting in a decrease of the workforce.

Biodegradable
Products or materials capable of being decayed by bacteria or other living organisms.

CFCs (chlorofluorocarbons)
A group of chemicals containing fluorine and chlorine, used in a variety of industries, which destroy ozone in the upper atmosphere.

Civil engineering
Engineering relating largely to the construction industry, for example roads, bridges and public buildings.

Colonization
The taking over of a less powerful country by more powerful countries.

Conserving
Using or managing a resource in such a way that it lasts for as long as possible.

Economist
Someone who is an expert in understanding business and finance.

Environmental impact
The impact or effect that a particular development process has on the environment.

Franchise
Permission to sell a company's goods or services on their behalf.

Gross Domestic Product (GDP)
The total amount of wealth produced by a country's industrial and economic activities.

Hydroelectricity
Electricity created by the use of water power.

Industrial relations
The relationship between managers and the workforce.

Industrial revolution
A period during the eighteenth and nineteenth centuries in which rapid mechanization took place.

Investment
Where individuals or organizations, including government, put money into a business or industry, either to support it or to receive a share of the profits.

Labour-intensive
Industries using large numbers of workers.

Mechanization
The introduction of machines to make manufacturing more efficient and (usually) less labour-intensive.

Mixed economy
A country's economy where there are both nationalized and privatized industries.

Nuclear waste
Radioactive by-products of nuclear power.

Primary energy sources
Sources of energy such as coal or oil which produce energy directly.

Prototype
The first of its kind to be made. Often used to detect faults before full-scale production starts.

Recession
A period of economic difficulty, which affects manufacturing, employment and other aspects of economic development.

Regional policies
Grants or other help given to regions to promote industry, employment and other development.

Restoration plan
A plan for the return of an area to its original state or different use, after it has served its industrial purpose.

Shareholders
Individuals or organizations who 'own' part of a business or industry by buying shares in it.

Subsidies
Grants or other financial help, usually given by government, to support a particular industry or sector of industry.

Turbines
Large propeller-like blades driven by steam or wind to make electricity.

Turnover
The total value of goods handled or sold rather than the actual profit made.

Value-added
The difference in value between the raw materials and the final product.

BOOKS TO READ

Business in Action: Coca Cola by William Gould (Cherrytree Books, 1995).

Exploring Industry by Cliff Lines (Wayland Publishers Ltd, 1987).

Industry in Europe by Mark Smalley (Wayland Publishers Ltd, 1992).

20th Century Industry by Rupert Matthews (Wayland Publishers Ltd, 1989).

INDEX